A Masterpiece of Moments

Rebecca Hume

BookLeaf Publishing

India | USA | UK

Presentation by *BookLeaf Publishing*

Web: www.bookleafpub.com

E-mail: info@bookleafpub.com

ISBN: 9789360949792

First edition 2024

*Avery, my wild child, my darling warrior - I
wrote this for you.*

ACKNOWLEDGEMENT

Thank you, God - for this child.

Thank you, Mom and Dad - for the love and the life that you have given me. I would not be the person or mother that I am today without your faith, wisdom, support, and affection.

Thank you, Amie - for knowing and loving every version of me.

Thank you, Sarah, Brittany, Sam, and Cohen - for being my tribe and my village on this wild and beautiful journey of motherhood. You are amazing mothers, sisters, and friends.

How blessed are we to be loved by you.

PREFACE

You are in every line I have ever written.

It is You

My darling warrior
Don't you know
It is you who tells the stars just where to go
It is you who sets the planets on their spin
And tells the night when to begin
It is you who shapes the clouds
With early morning light
Demands the sun to shine
And birds to take their flight
Who tells the breeze to stay or leave
And the flowers what to believe
My darling warrior
It is you
Who turns the night sky to light blue
And meets the dawning day with your kiss
To say… it is this. It is this.

That the sun might rise and set with you
Of my doubts, I carry few

It is you
It is you
Where dreams might only just come true
Where fragile hope might dare to bloom
It is you

It is you

Home

2

I had not known it then
But never could unknow again
The space inside of me
Between my blood and bones
That was fated to be filled
When first you called me home

Here is Your Child

Here is the warmth of the sun
From both sides
Here is more beauty
Than one heart could hold

Here is the deepest river running
Here is every star in the sky
Here is where the ocean meets the shore
Here is every whispered reason why

Here is the shine beneath the rust
Here is the glory between dust to dust
Here is everything you ever wanted
Here is everything you never knew

Here is your ancestors' masterpiece
Here is your most sacred dream
Here is your unbroken hallelujah
Here is your prayer laid at the Lord's feet

Here is the reward for daydream believing
Here is your consolation for all of life's leaving
Here is victory o'er every demon ever wrestled
Here is your life's meaning, in one tiny vessel

All Reason

My soul whispered your name
Before you were formed
And though my heart knew not
What she was missing
In the darkest nights did mourn
With a longing, quietly sharp and undefined
Until the moment
You were called mine

Until your skin on my skin
Your blood in my vein
The sound and soul and shape of you
Cracked me open
With the weight of fullness
And primal claim became
The only sound I knew

And all reason man has ever given
To tread this vast and wild earth
At once made sense to me
The moment of your birth

That I'd known joy and love and grace, if ever,
Was paled the moment our two souls tethered

One

Just one second's blazing glory
Just one page within your story
Just one note of your tiny voice
No cadence, context, would I rejoice

And if my final breath were offered
Wishes, magic, fortunes proffered
I would ask for just this only grant
One more time to hold your hand

Present

Be here now, the incessant mantra
Constantly it plays
Backbeat to the steady rhythm
Of our groundhog days

I swear that I am present
I am here inside these moments
I memorize your sweet, small voice
And your silly laughter
Mark and save their sound and cadence
Replayed forever after

Photograph in my mind
The light through windowpanes
Your sleepy eyes and nap wild hair
The gentle curve of your face

I swear I see it, I save it all
I swear I hold and savor
Every fleeting moment's seconds
Every God granted simple favor

I carve it all in stone
Every little piece and part
Within the book of memories

I store inside my heart

And am but slightly desperate
In how overly aware
That I shall never get it back
When now becomes then
And here becomes there

And for the very life of me
I cannot find nor fathom
How the life of you, of us
So quickly by it passes

And have yet to sort it out
To grace or comprehend
How to celebrate each new chapter
Lest I mourn the one that ends

Midnights

I remember the long nights in the early days
Midnight lives spent in your room
Eternal hours in a secret world
Just the stars and me and you

I remember when it was soft and quiet
As though time stopped outside your window
In the magic of our newness
The winter's first and falling snow

And I remember just as well
Exhausted tears from both our eyes
On nights no rest was offered
Each attempt a new reprise

As I begged for granted grace
Those nights that felt unending
I feigned the fortitude you needed
With my best pretending

I imagined I was an actress
Playing the role of Tired Mother
With aching bones and soothing lines
One take after another

Our survival scene on repeat
I'd hush and nurse and hold you
Whispering the moon's sweet lullabies
The script that might console you

Until at last you rested
Wet lashes kissed your cheek
The weight of you, love's lifeline
My child, mild and meak

And when we cut to morning
With gentle rays of early sun
I knew one day even this I'd miss
Our tiny battles won

Symphony of My Soul

You are the symphony of my soul
Beating through my heart
Crescendos bright and full
Each harmony in part

Your melody sustains me
It's ever changing timbre
A song so wild and free
With notes of sweet November

We are tethered by its tune
Each chord that tells your story
A harmony in bloom
Life's soundtrack full of glory

To Be Your Mother

To be your shelter and your teacher
Make safe your childhood nest
Just to watch you fly into the world
My lessons each to test

What joy and fear to watch you soar
As I pray the Lord to guide you
That you stand back up each time you fall
His and my love right beside you

This golden chapter that I have you
Granted far too short a loan
To shape and raise and celebrate you
As you become your own

Tiny Clothes

I dress you in these tiny clothes
And still cannot believe
That an entire future fits inside
Each little leg and sleeve

How blessed am I to witness
To watch you as you grow
Albeit bittersweetness
That time I cannot slow

Vows

This promise to you I bring
For more sacred vows could not exist
Than the ones I whisper nightly
As your lovely face I kiss

There is no greater fear nor love
Than these I carry now for you
And nothing on the Lord's green earth
For you, I would not do

I would wage the greatest wars
Or wash the feet of enemies
If either one could serve you best
To wrap your life in peace

This Chapter

This chapter you won't remember
All this magic and delight
For at least one more December
Like daydreams fading into night

They are but gifts for only me
Every word and step and kiss
Softly slipping past your memory
To dwell inside my solo reminisce

Every toddler hard flung hug
Every sticky hand-held stroll
Every Sunday snuggle bug
Every rock and every roll

A forgotten era of just us two
In a world built all our own
I'll carry them instead for you
All these days we've grown

And soon the things we do together
Your mind will learn to save
But I shall cherish now forever
Every secret moment of these days

Self

They say you lose yourself in motherhood
Become a different person
But the me I am with you
Is my favorite version

And oh, I don't forget her
The girl I used to be
Sometimes I wish you'd met her
To know all sides of me

Instead I'll take the lessons earned
In every far-gone stage
The things I've loved and lost and learned
The tears and try-agains upon each page

Host and harness them to guide me
In this new life that I was made for
And of every past version inside of me
I will forever love you more

Prayer

Lord, let no harm befall this child
Make him brave
And leave him wild

Keep him sweet and keep him kind
A beauty seeker
So joy he'll find

Let him always know love, Lord
And reflect it to others
Both in his deed and his word

And guard him from the dangers
Of heartache from friends
And malice from strangers

Give him strength and fortitude
Through any darkness
Your light in him exude

And Lord, give him my whole heart
That he'll always carry me with him
Long years after we must part

The Poetry of Us

These words that I have written
And rewritten
Again and again and again
On pages of my past
Long before we began

I heard their quiet echo
Every day and every night
But never could I find
Where they each belonged
Their rhythm and their rhyme

Until the day I became yours
And you mine
And every word and every space
Became the poetry of us
Each line in perfect place

In Another Life

If there was another world
One without a me and you
I think I'd find you anyway
And love you when I do

I'd say I know you somehow
That you bring to mind
A faded photo in my pocket
From a long, lost other time

My soul would light up
With the sweetest recognition
The other half of me
Two hearts without division

Your Face

I had a vision once
When you were but a seed
Of an older you
Who turned and smiled at me

Long and lanky
Not quite grown
Standing at the back door
Of some future home

He had the same blue eyes
That you came into this world with
Your tousled brown hair
And a young man's chin

I think I see him sometimes
In the curve of your cheek
The dimple in your smile
Your mouth when you speak

I see him then and see you now
Just as I always see
Your newborn face today
And everything between

And now I know the secret
That every mother can
Still see her babe's first face
Even when he is a man

What I'll Tell You

Brush your teeth
Make you bed
Don't forget to pray

Always tell the truth
Be kind to others
Balance work and play

Stand up tall
Hold your head high
Give grace a place to stay

Find joy in kindness
Add generosity and laughter
To the beauty of each day

Know yourself
And know God too
So you'll never lose your way

But if you do
Come back to me
And I'll love the loss away

I Knew You First

You came to me like summer
From behind spring's façade
Like gentle twilight slumber
In a world that time forgot

I think I knew you first
Before I knew myself
So full of love and thirst
A need I'd never felt

That turned inside of me
Pieces I'd yet to find
Sunshine and rain a symphony
Our destinies entwined

Painting

If I could paint a picture
To put on full display
The magnitude by which I love you
That words fall short to say

I'd paint the sky the color of your eyes
Blue and bright and bold
So yourself you'd recognize
In the hue it holds

I'd paint the ocean vast and wide
Waves rising in the air
Rolling with the changing tide
Curls like your beach blown hair

I'd paint the tiny treasures
Along the sparkling shore
The sea's cacophony of endless pleasures
Washed from the ocean's floor

I'd paint birds speckled in the sky
Heron, piper, and seagull
Quietly majestic as they fly by
Their hearts and bellies full

I'd paint the sun as brightly as you shine
Light reflecting a million rays of beauty
Your mirrored magic marked divine
My infinite affection, deeper than the sea

Enough

25

If this is all there is to life
The sun filtering in
Through the leaves in the yard
The beat of your heart
And your weight in my arms
Your small feet on the hardwood
My name on your lips
"Mama, Mama" and your sweet kiss
If there was never more
To do or say or see
This masterpiece of moments
Would be enough for me